Baker Street Whodunits

Baker Street Whodunits

Tom Bullimore

Illustrated by Ian Anderson

Sterling Publishing Co. Inc.
New York

Library of Congress Cataloging-in-Publication Data

Bullimore, Tom.
  Baker Street whodunits / Tom Bullimore ; illustrated by Ian Anderson.
    p.   cm.
  Includes index.
  ISBN 0-8069-4763-2
    1. Puzzles. 2. Detective and mystery stories. 3. Doyle, Arthur Conan, Sir,
  1859–1930—Characters—Sherlock Holmes. I. Anderson, Ian. II. Title.
  GV1507.D4 B855 2001
  793.73—dc21   2001020196

10 9 8

Published by Sterling Publishing Co., Inc.
387 Park Avenue South, New York, NY 10016
© 2001 by Tom Bullimore
Distributed in Canada by Sterling Publishing
℅ Canadian Manda Group, 165 Dufferin Street
Toronto, Ontario, Canada M6K 3H6
Distributed in Great Britain and Europe by Chris Lloyd at Orca Book
Services, Stanley House, Fleets Lane, Poole BH15 3AJ, England
Distributed in Australia by Capricorn Link (Australia) Pty. Ltd.
P.O. Box 704, Windsor, NSW 2756, Australia

Sterling ISBN 0-8069-4763-2

For information about custom editions, special sales, premium and
corporate purchases, please contact Sterling Special Sales
Department at 800-805-5489 or specialsales@sterlingpub.com.

Sherlock Holmes and Doctor Watson went for a game of golf. Fortunately, the course was fairly quiet and only a few other golfers were waiting to play. Holmes, Watson, and two other golfers decided to play together as a foursome. During the course of the game Holmes discovered that one of the golfers was the father of the other golfer's son.

Can you deduce how the two golfers were related?

"Professor Moriarty has robbed three houses on Elmore Street—Numbers 8, 12, and 18," Doctor Watson informed Sherlock Holmes. "I wonder which house he will rob tonight."

Holmes smiled. "My dear Watson," he said, "I know exactly which house the old fox will rob."

Do you know?

A robber carrying a bag of stolen money came rushing around a corner of London Docks with Sherlock Holmes some fifty yards back in pursuit. On seeing the fully laden ferry some ten feet from the jetty, the robber increased his speed dramatically. As he approached the edge of the jetty, he hurled the bag toward the ferry and looked on as it landed with a dull thud on the deck. He then quickly took several paces back and sprinted forward, hurling himself like a champion long jumper toward the vessel. Landing facedown on the deck, he turned and smiled at the great detective. A man helped the robber to his feet and said a few words to him. The smile on the robber's face turned to despair.

What did the man say to cause the robber's change of mood?

At long last Sherlock Holmes had brought Professor Moriarty to trial for a capital offense. As Holmes looked on, sitting in the back of the courtroom, the judge and the jury found his old adversary guilty, and the judge was about to pronounce sentence. Moriarty interrupted the judge and asked to make one more statement. The judge agreed and gave him the following choice: If his statement was true he would be hanged; if it was false he would be shot by a firing squad. A wry smile crossed the face of Sherlock Holmes as Moriarty made a statement that made it impossible to execute him. What did Moriarty say?

Sherlock Holmes and Doctor Watson stood looking down at the dead body of Lord Foxley.

"I wonder what time he was murdered," said Watson.

At that moment, His Lordship's somewhat forgetful butler stepped forward. "I know exactly when he was murdered," he announced. "I was in my bathroom shaving when I heard the shot. I recall looking in my mirror and the time on the clock behind me said 20 minutes to 10."

What was the correct time of His Lordship's death?

Through the excellent work of Sherlock Holmes and his colleague Doctor Watson, three criminals had been brought to court. They stood in the dock together. Bloggs stood to the left of Norman (though not necessarily next to him). Norman stood to the right of Doe. Fred stood to the left of Archie. Archie stood to the left of Fiddle.

Can you match all three surnames with the correct first name?

Doctor Watson searched his desk for a box of matches with which to light his pipe. To his amazement, he found four unused boxes. Watson noticed that on the side of each box was written AVERAGE CONTENTS 50 MATCHES. Out of curiosity, he counted the contents of each box and discovered that the average contents was indeed 50. If box A had one more match than box B, but seven less than box C, which had nine more than box D, how many matches did each box contain?

Professor Moriarty had taken Sherlock Holmes, Doctor Watson, and Inspector Lestrade hostage. After a few hours, the Professor entered the room where they were bound by rope and blindfolded all three. Moriarty then made the following announcement: "I have in my possession five caps—two red and three white. I'm now going to place a cap on each of your heads."

On doing this, Moriarty removed the blindfolds from Watson and Lestrade. He then asked Watson if he could identify conclusively the color of the cap on his head and added that if he got it wrong he would shoot him. Watson wasn't prepared to answer. He then asked Lestrade the same question; Lestrade was also not prepared to answer. Moriarty laughed and was about to leave the room when the still blindfolded Holmes spoke.

"If I can tell you the color of the cap on my head, will you release all three of us?" Moriarty agreed. Holmes duly answered correctly without his blindfold being removed.

Can you deduce how Holmes did this?

Sherlock Holmes received the following note:

"I will <u>slate</u> <u>icons</u> from the <u>potsstream</u> on <u>dynamo</u>."

After underlining five of the words, he handed the note to Watson.

"By Jove," said Watson. "It doesn't make sense, old boy."

"Exactly," replied Holmes. "That's why I underlined those particular words. They are anagrams of the true words in the note. Even you, Watson, should be able to rearrange them and make sense of the statement."

Can you?

Sherlock Holmes was explaining to Doctor Watson that he must take care when reading any documented evidence, lest important details were overlooked.

"For example," said Holmes, "how many times will you read the following short story before you solve the question?"

He handed Watson a notepad on which was written:

Patricia was 21 years old, six years older than her sister Brenda, whose only brother's mother's only sister was 10 years older than Patricia and was called Marigold. Marigold's brother, who was nine years older than her, was her sister's twin. If Brenda's brother Michael was 19 years younger than Marigold's brother Ian, how was Michael related to Patricia?

Can you find the answer?

Sherlock Holmes was set upon by three thugs as he returned to 221b Baker Street one winter's evening. From the following information, can you identify each attacker, his nickname, and the weapon he carried?

1. Grant, who didn't have the nickname Buster, carried the club.
2. Basher carried the knife.
3. O'Shea didn't have the crowbar.
4. Parker didn't have the nickname Knuckles.

Sherlock Holmes and Doctor Watson were playing cards for pennies, and Watson was having by far the best of the duel, leaving Holmes with only 12 of his original 50 pennies.

"I would like to set you a task, Watson," said Holmes. "And if you should succeed, my remaining 12 pennies will be yours. But if you should fail, then you will return all the pennies you have won from me."

"Sounds fair, Holmes," said Watson.

"Then I want you to take my 12 pennies and place them on the table so that they form six rows with four coins in each row."

Watson couldn't do it. Perhaps you can do better.

A man had weights attached to his ankles and had been partially buried—standing upright—in the sand on a quiet, lonely beach to await his fate when the tide came in. Thankfully, he was rescued in time by Sherlock Holmes. If at the time of his discovery $\frac{1}{6}$ of his body was buried beneath the sand, while another $\frac{2}{3}$ was covered by water, and the remaining 13 inches (32.5cm) were above water, how tall was the man?

Lord Finchley had been assaulted in his study by an unseen attacker. The attack left him unconscious for some 20 minutes, and when he recovered, he discovered that his safe had been broken into and a large sum of money had disappeared. Lord Finchley immediately made four phone calls—to Sherlock Holmes, Inspector Lestrade, his accountant, and his doctor, all of whom rushed to the scene. If Holmes arrived before the accountant but behind the doctor, and Lestrade arrived before the accountant but behind Holmes, in which order did they arrive at Finchley Manor?

Sherlock Holmes entered a sporting goods store and purchased a pair of hiking boots and a compass. In total, they cost him £22.50. If the hiking boots cost £18.50 more than the compass, how much did they each cost?

Sherlock Holmes sent Doctor Watson the following teaser:

COWMOS   BULSTAIN   PEAGHNCONE   GOWSLAG

SHELIKIN   SHETAN   BRIDEHUNG   NONOLD

Each of the scrambled words, when unscrambled, will spell out the name of a city visited recently by a detective colleague of Holmes.

"One of the cities is a red herring—disregard it and you can spell out the first name of the detective," Holmes informed Watson.

Can you identify the cities and the name of the detective?

Three of the nurses who worked at the hospital where Doctor Watson was doing some charity work were close friends. They worked the night duty on adjacent wards. All three were married, but only one of them to a doctor. Doctor Watson asked Sherlock Holmes to work out the full name of each nurse, the ward in which she worked, and her husband's occupation. He gave Holmes the following information to assist him. Can you work it out?

1. Nancy worked in the ward next to Mrs. Jones, whose husband was an undertaker.
2. Mrs. Smithson worked on a ward numbered lower than the ward of Barbara, whose husband wasn't the cab driver.
3. Audrey worked in ward four and not in ward six.
4. Mrs. Green did not work in ward two.

Sherlock Holmes, Doctor Watson, and Inspector Lestrade all entered a barber shop for a haircut and a shave. There were two barbers, who both worked at the same speed, and they boasted that it took them only 18 minutes to complete a haircut and six minutes to complete a shave. This being the case, what would be the minimum time it would take them to deal with our three friends?

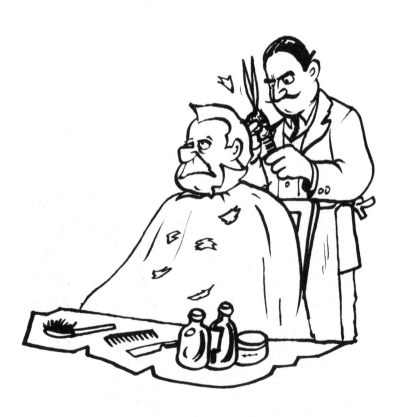

Inspector Lestrade was about to introduce Sherlock Holmes and Doctor Watson to three ladies at a charity function.

"Before you introduce us," Watson said confidently, "allow me to use my powers of deduction and identify all three of them."

"Go ahead, Watson," said Holmes.

"Lady Agatha is the redhead. Lady Jane has the gray hair, and Lady Davina is the blonde," Watson said proudly.

"Completely wrong," replied Lestrade.

Watson frowned. Holmes leaned over and whispered in his colleague's ear. "It may assist you, Watson, if I were to tell you that I just overheard the blonde asking one of the others, 'How are you enjoying the party, Lady Agatha?'"

Can you identify which color hair each of the three ladies had?

Sherlock Holmes and Doctor Watson were sitting by a roaring fire at 221b Baker Street. Holmes puffed on his pipe and then broke the silence.

"Yesterday, Watson, I walked north for over a minute, but I had actually moved further south."

"Great Scot, Holmes, that's impossible!" exclaimed Watson.

"Not so, Watson," replied Holmes.

Can you deduce how Holmes achieved this?

Sherlock Holmes noted the following riddle written on a wall:

What am I?
My first is in bone but not in home,
My second is in nurse and also in purse,
My third is in rob and also in robe,
My fourth is in angle but not in bevel,
My fifth is in ladder and also in bladder,
My sixth is in rabbit and also in habit,
My seventh is in prison but not in jail.

Can you provide the answer?

Sherlock Holmes has four different colors of gloves in his dresser drawer. Two pairs are black, three pairs are white, four pairs are blue, and five pairs are brown.

How many gloves must he take out of the drawer to be certain of having a matching pair?

Working on the case of the gold balls that were missing from a London museum, Holmes's detective work led him into the Italian Alps. There he discovered the gold balls in the possession of a gang of dangerous criminals. When the opportunity presented itself, Holmes recovered the balls and was pursued through the mountains by the gang. Suddenly Holmes found himself at a ravine over which was a rather shaky-looking bridge. On the bridge was a sign that declared the maximum weight to cross at one time was 183 pounds. Holmes knew that he weighed exactly 168 pounds, while the gold balls weighed 10 pounds each. Holmes quickly thought about the situation, and then made his way safely to the other side of the bridge with the two balls.

How did he get across?

Sherlock Holmes glanced up from his evening newspaper.

"Dick Powers, the gang leader who was responsible for all that trouble down at the docks, has been found dead," he said to Doctor Watson.

"How old was he, Holmes?" asked Watson.

"Well, he was 34 years old when his youngest son was born, and his eldest son, who was six years older than the youngest, was 40 on the day of his death," Holmes answered.

Can you deduce the age of Dick Powers at his death?

Sherlock Holmes passed a notepad to his colleague Doctor Watson. On it was written the following:

A PURGE
B GRAZE
C THREES
D MARDI

"Unravel each of these, Watson, to reveal a European town or city. In one of these I believe we will find Professor Moriarty," said Holmes with a sardonic smile.

Can you do it?

Doctor Watson was telling Sherlock Holmes about his niece Anne Amelia Forsythe. He said Amelia (she preferred the name Amelia to Anne) went to Liverpool (a city she liked better than London), where she met two men. She was attracted to David (not Keith), and made a date to meet him the following day. She preferred to meet him at noon (as opposed to eleven, as he suggested). David then suggested a number of activities for the afternoon—punting, walking, golfing, tennis, and riding.

"Now," said Watson confidently, "can you deduce which activity my niece chose?"

Holmes answered correctly almost immediately. Can you do the same?

While working on the case of a bank break-in, Sherlock Holmes, Doctor Watson, and Inspector Lestrade took time out to compare notes on the evidence discovered so far.

Holmes stated that he had found the crowbar that was used to break into the bank, and that Watson had discovered the fingerprints on the vault.

Watson stated that Lestrade had found the crowbar and that Holmes had found the bundle of used banknotes.

Lestrade stated that Holmes had found the fingerprints and that Watson had found the crowbar.

As it turned out, only one of the three was correct in both statements, while another was correct in one statement and wrong in the other, and the third was completely wrong in both statements.

Can you deduce exactly who found what?

While being tracked down by Sherlock Holmes, Professor Moriarty, Fingers Malloy, and Shifty White carried out a total of 49 robberies between them. If Moriarty committed twice as many robberies as Malloy, who in turn carried out twice as many robberies as White, how many robberies did each of the three commit?

Sherlock Holmes and Doctor Watson were part of a team of criminologists participating in a charity walk. From the following information, can you deduce each team's placement in the event?

The team from Scotland Yard finished ahead of the team of lawyers, but behind the criminologists. The team of journalists finished ahead of the team of doctors, but behind the team of lawyers.

What was the order of finish?

Sherlock Holmes set out this puzzle for Watson, using the following numbers only: 10, 8, 6, 4, and 2.

?	6	6	2	8	= 16
4	?	10	10	4	= 15
6	2	?	8	8	= 13
10	8	6	?	4	= 16
8	8	6	6	?	= 19

Can you identify the missing numbers?

Doctor Watson was rather depressed as he and Sherlock Holmes traveled back to London by hansom cab after a day at the races.

"I'll never gamble again," Watson stated. "That's £35 I lost today."

"Let me try and take your mind off all that, Watson," said Holmes. "Here are some letters grouped together with the vowels removed. Can you insert the vowels and form a well known proverb?"

FLND HSMN YRSN PRTD.

Can you decipher it?

Sherlock Holmes and Doctor Watson had apprehended a well known pickpocket and escorted him to the nearest police station, where he was asked to empty his pockets. Much to their chagrin, his pockets contained nothing that could link him to any crime. He laid on the table six items in all (see diagram below). From the following information, can you work out the position of each item on the table?

1	2	3
4	5	6

1. The comb was on the bottom row directly below the pen knife.

2. The gold coin was directly to the left of the box of matches and directly above the key.

3. The pencil was directly to the left of the comb.

Sherlock Holmes discovered that four stolen items, from a case that he was working on, had been sold to members of a club in Mayfair. The four items were sold for a total cost of £400. The gold watch was sold for twice the price of the necklace. The ring was sold for the same amount as the watch and the necklace combined, and the bracelet went for twice the price of the gold watch.

Can you determine the selling price of each of the four items?

Sherlock Holmes and Doctor Watson entered the courtroom where four criminals, known as Fingers, Hatchet Jack, Big Al, and Greasy Harry, were seated together in the dock awaiting sentence. They sat in a straight line.

"I've never seen any of them before, but I'm sure I can identify all four," announced Watson.

"Go ahead," said Holmes.

"The one on the far left is Fingers; next to him is Greasy Harry. On the far right is Hatchet Jack with Big Al on his left."

"Completely wrong, Watson. Not one correct," said Holmes.

"Then Greasy Harry is on the far right, with Fingers on his left; Big Al is on the far left, with Hatchet Jack on his right," he announced with confidence.

"Completely wrong again," replied Holmes with a smile.

"Then Hatchet Jack is second from the right and Big Al is second from the left!" Watson snapped.

But he was completely wrong again. Can you work out the seating positions of each man from left to right?

Sherlock Holmes asked Doctor Watson to unravel the following anagrams to identify four occupations Professor Moriarty may have chosen for his latest escapade.

1. Peek one nest
2. Mail ponce
3. Heard risers
4. Pilot in CIA

Can you do it?

While practicing on the shooting range at Scotland Yard, Inspector Lestrade scored ten points less than Doctor Watson. Sergeant Black scored 15 more points than Doctor Watson, but 25 less than Sherlock Holmes. If, between them, they scored a total of 425 points, how many points did they each score?

Sherlock Holmes found himself in a small hamlet in Kent as he traced the whereabouts of a notorious criminal. On his arrival, he spoke with one of the locals.

"How long have you lived here?" he asked the man.

"Well, sir, let me see now," the man replied. "My father's mother was born here some 130 years past. She had her first-born, my uncle Tom, 20 years after that, and he was three years older than my aunt Vi, who was two years older than my father, her brother. When my father was a young man of 35, he wed young Mary Butterfield from Upminster. She had three sons—one after the other—two years after being wed, and three years, and four years after—she died giving birth to me, sir, and I've lived here ever since."

From the above, can you work out the age of the man Holmes was speaking to?

As Sherlock Holmes and Doctor Watson strolled through Clapham Common, Holmes asked Watson the following:

"If ONE is worth four, TWO worth three, THREE worth two, FOUR worth 7, and FIVE worth 3, what are SIX and SEVEN worth?"

Watson had no answer for this. Perhaps you can do better.

Both Sherlock Holmes and Doctor Watson were great lovers of the Englishman's favorite refreshment—tea. If Holmes himself went through a pound of tea in 12 days, and when joined with Watson, went through a pound in four days, how many days would it take Watson to go through a pound of tea on his own?

Sherlock Holmes was about to call upon and interview four witnesses who had seen a violent crime take place. From the following information, can you deduce the occupation of each and give the street where he or she lived?

1. Mr. Black, who did not live on Hay Street, was neither the banker nor the baker.
2. The gentleman who lived on Law Street was the engineer.
3. Neither Mr. Shell nor Mrs. Carr lived on Able Street.
4. Mr. Cook wasn't the grocer, nor did he live on Bright Street or Law Street.
5. The grocer lived on Able Street.
6. The person who got the closest look at the criminal felt certain that he recognized the man as the one who had called at his residence on Hay Street only a few days before, posing as a salesman.
7. The banker didn't live on Bright Street.

"Try this, Watson," said Sherlock Holmes to Doctor Watson, who sat opposite him in the study of 221b Baker Street. "Here are 20 words. What I want you to do is join two words together to make one word, so that you end up with ten words instead of 20. You must use each word only once."

The 20 words were:

CHAR	BREAK	BEND
HOT	ROAD	SHOP
ABLE	SHOT	TING
BACK	OUT	CAST
BANK	WORK	LIFT
LAW	SET	FAST
NOTE	AWAY	

Can you do it?

Holmes was working on a robbery case, and in order to further his investigations, he needed to know how long it would take the average man to run from the bank in Windsor Street to Kings Cross Railway Station. He timed himself, Doctor Watson, and Inspector Lestrade. The combined total of their times was one hour and 11 minutes. If Holmes was seven minutes faster than Watson, who was three minutes slower than Lestrade, how long did it take each of them to complete the distance?

The following four words have been jumbled up. They are part of a code used by the infamous Professor Moriarty. Holmes discovered them while on the trail of his greatest adversary. Can you unscramble the letters and find the words?

1. TCORPAKC
2. GYNATCTN
3. TWAAOICST
4. EJFAICNKK

"Ah, Watson!" exclaimed Holmes, as his colleague entered the study of 221b. "Now that you're back, perhaps you can give me the last two letters in this sequence, which appeared on a scrap of paper that had been found in Professor Moriarty's rooms."

TEERTSREK

Watson didn't have a clue, do you?

Sherlock Holmes and Doctor Watson stood in the Tate Gallery, admiring the paintings of some of the greatest artists in the world.

"This is amazing," said Watson. "This is the first time I've been inside an art gallery."

Holmes, of course, had visited many galleries in many different cities. From the lists below, can you match up the galleries with the cities in which they are located?

Galleries: Hermitage, Prado, Rijksmuseum, the National Gallery, the Louvre.

Cities: Madrid, Paris, Leningrad, Amsterdam, Dublin.

Sherlock Holmes had been responsible for the eventual capture of four criminals, Higgins, Hart, Fish, and Brown, who had robbed the country house of Lord Archer. From the following information, can you match each criminal with his first name and identify the items in his possession at the time of his arrest?

1. Lance didn't have the diamonds, nor was his surname Brown.
2. Higgins had the silver, which he was intending to share with Simon, whose surname wasn't Hart.
3. Bob, whose surname wasn't Fish, didn't have the money, nor did he have the gold.
4. Tom, who was neither Hart nor Brown, didn't have either the gold or the diamonds.
5. Lance and the person with the gold were cousins.
6. Brown didn't have the money or the gold.

Lord Fanshaw was having a statue of himself erected outside his country mansion, but a problem arose regarding the mounting of the statue on a pedestal, so His Lordship sent for Sherlock Holmes.

"You see, Holmes," said Lord Fanshaw when the great detective arrived, "the statue weighs five tons, and the only way it can be lifted is by a crane and two slings under the base. The problem is—how do we set the statue down on the pedestal and get the slings out?"

Holmes gave the matter some thought and came up with a solution in four minutes. Can you find one?

"Try this one, Holmes," said Doctor Watson with confidence. "Change the word BOOK to CASE by changing one letter at a time. Each change must result in another English word. I managed it in six moves. Can you equal that?"

Holmes achieved it in five moves. Can you?

During a murder inquiry aboard an express train, Sherlock Holmes spoke with three of the suspects—Mr. Butcher, Mr. Baker, and Mr. Banks—who, as it turned out, were a butcher, a baker, and a banker by profession. From this conversation, Holmes was given the following facts:

1. Mr. Butcher is not the baker.
2. Mr. Baker is not the banker.
3. Mr. Butcher is the butcher.
4. Mr. Banks is not the banker.

Looking more closely at these statements, Holmes discovered that only one of them was true. He was then able to deduce the true occupation of each of the men. Can you?

Sherlock Holmes had been given charge of three boxes. One box contained two diamonds, another contained one diamond and one emerald, and the third two emeralds. For identification purposes, the boxes were labeled DD, DE, and EE. But, as it turned out, a mix-up took place, and no box contained the correct combination as indicated on the label. This being the case, what is the smallest number of precious stones that can be removed from the boxes in order to identify the contents of each?

Professor Moriarty entered a second-hand furniture shop and purchased a mahogany bookcase for £25, which he paid for by check. He then had second thoughts about the bookcase and exchanged it for a writing table that cost £15. Because the shop owner did not have enough cash in the till, he cashed Moriarty's check with the owner of the shop next door and gave Moriarty £10 in change. As you would expect from Professor Moriarty, the check eventually bounced, and the shop owner had to borrow £25 to repay the shop owner next door. If the writing table cost the second-hand furniture dealer £11, how much did he lose?

Following a grisly murder, Sherlock Holmes interviewed four of the staff at Hammers Hall—the butler, the gardener, the chef, and the stable boy. From the following information, can you match the surnames with the correct first names and occupations of the four hired hands?

1. Tom, whose surname was neither Brown nor Jones, was the butler.
2. The gardener's first name was neither Jack nor John.
3. Smith's first name wasn't Tim.
4. Small was either the stable boy or the gardener.
5. Tim and Brown were cousins.
6. The chef and John were good friends.
7. Jones was neither the stable boy nor the gardener.

Sherlock Holmes was being held prisoner in a dark dungeon by the evil Professor Moriarty. He found 64 candle stubs lying on the dungeon floor. He could make one full candle from four stubs, and one candle would burn down to a stub in one hour.

Working on the theory that Holmes could only light full candles, how many hours of candlelight would he have before being left in total darkness?

Before being apprehended by Sherlock Holmes, Professor Moriarty had conned a number of people out of a total of £3895 in one particular scam. Each person had lost the same amount of money to the evil professor. If there were more than 50 people, but less than 100 involved in the scam, can you work out exactly how many people were conned by the Professor and how much they each lost?

Sherlock Holmes and Doctor Watson were sitting in a restaurant.

"Behind you, Watson," said Holmes, "are three ladies sitting together at a table. I have observed that between them they are wearing a total of 14 rings on their fingers. One is wearing twice as many as another, and one more than the third. Without turning around, tell me how many rings each one is wearing."

Can you work it out?

"Here's one for you, Watson," announced Sherlock Holmes. "Here are nine words:

ION	BAN	RAN
A	KING	PRO
SAC	DON	BAT

From these nine words, I want you to make three words. In each case, the word is made up by combining three of the aforementioned words. Naturally, you can use each of the nine words only once."

Can you do it?

While taking a long train journey, Sherlock Holmes dealt six cards faceup in a straight line before starting a form of solitaire. From the following information, can you identify the six cards as they read from left to right?

1. The six cards were: 10 of clubs, 9 of hearts, 10 of spades, Queen of diamonds, 9 of clubs, and 7 of diamonds.
2. None of the cards were in the order indicated above.
3. Both diamonds were to the left of the spade.
4. The 9 of clubs had a red card directly on either side of it.
5. The heart had the spade directly to its left and a club directly to its right.
6. The 7 was to the left of the Queen.

Four men sat around a table in a London pub. Unknown to them they were being keenly observed by the master of disguise—Sherlock Holmes. Some time later, Holmes was joined by his good friend Doctor Watson.

"Have they divulged any information on the murder, Holmes?" Watson whispered.

"Indeed, Watson," replied Holmes with a smile.

"Then who is the murderer?" asked Watson enthusiastically.

"Ha! That is what I want you to tell me," said Holmes. "Brush away those cobwebs and put your brain into action."

Holmes then relayed the following information to the good doctor. Can you deduce just which of the four was the murderer?

1. Tom Cobley sat to the right of the man eating steak and kidney pie.
2. John Smith sat directly opposite the man eating fish.
3. The fish eater sat to the right of the chicken eater.
4. Frank Simkins was not eating steak and kidney pie.
5. John Fern was to the left of the man eating lamb chops.
6. The fish eater confessed to the murder.

Lord Cavell looked across at Sherlock Holmes and shook his head. "It's a most disturbing set of events, Holmes," he said.

Holmes agreed. "Correct me if I'm wrong, my lord," he said, "but these items were stolen from your household on different days?"

"Without question, Holmes," Lord Cavell replied. "The cuff links were stolen before the diamond tie pin, but two days after the gold lighter. The watch chain was stolen after the gold lighter but before the cigar box—which was stolen the day before the tie pin. The question is, which blighter on my staff would do such a thing?"

Holmes would undoubtedly resolve the whole affair, but the order in which the items were stolen was of prime importance in the solution.

Can you deduce what that order was?

Sherlock Holmes glanced up from his copy of *The Times* and spoke to Doctor Watson. "Retract . . . A sweet juice . . . easy gallop . . . altered state," he said.

"Have you gone crazy, Holmes?" asked Watson. "You're speaking gibberish."

"Not so, Watson," replied Holmes. "I have just recited four clues from today's crossword. The amazing thing is that the four answers are all made up using the same six letters."

Can you identify the four answers to Holmes's crossword?

As Sherlock Holmes and Doctor Watson sat in the witness room of the Old Bailey where they were to give evidence for the prosecution in a murder case, Holmes gave Watson the following problem to solve to relieve the boredom.

"Take these four words: ENDS HOLE RAYS and ABLE. Now find one four-letter word that can be added to the front of these words, making four eight-letter words."

By the time they were called into the witness stand, Watson had failed to supply the answer.

Can you do it?

Winston Kelp was something of a daredevil burglar who thought he was a great deal smarter than Sherlock Holmes. Late one afternoon he sent a telegram to the great detective announcing that he would rob three houses in Rawlings Street that very evening. He supplied Holmes with the door numbers of 12 houses: 25, 27, 3, 12, 9, 15, 6, 30, 21, and 19. The telegram concluded with a further announcement that the total of all three houses he intended to rob would be 50.

Like Holmes, can you quickly deduce the three houses that would be robbed?

Sherlock Holmes apprehended three young pickpockets who were busy working Shepherd's Bush market. Their total combined ages were 33 years. If Ted was twice the age of Martin, and three times the age of Henry, how old was each of the three pickpockets?

Doctor Watson's pocket watch was correct at midday, but then it began to gain two and a half minutes every hour. If it stopped two hours ago, showing a quarter past six, what time should Watson's timepiece be showing?

Sherlock Holmes, Doctor Watson, and Inspector Lestrade were all enjoying a Sunday morning fishing on the Thames, when suddenly someone fired a gun from the opposite bank. If Lestrade heard the gun go off with a loud bang, and Watson saw the splash as the bullet hit the water, while Holmes saw the smoke rising from the gun—who was first and who was last to become aware of the shot?

Sherlock Holmes had followed a mysterious member of the underworld fraternity, whom he knew only by the nickname "Gofar." Holmes saw him enter a gunsmith's shop. In order to get a better view of the proceedings, Holmes casually strolled up to the shop window and gazed in. What he saw being purchased immediately aroused his interest. Gofar was purchasing an assortment of shotguns, handguns, and packs of ammunition. These were divided into five separate parcels and charged separately:

1. Two shotguns and two handguns cost £26.
2. A handgun, two packs of ammunition, and a shotgun cost £31.
3. Four packs of ammunition cost £36.
4. A handgun and three packs of ammunition cost £35.
5. Holmes could not see the fifth parcel clearly, but he noted that it was something packed together with three packs of ammunition at a price of £32.

What was the item that Holmes could not identify in the fifth parcel?

In a warehouse, Sherlock Holmes found a number of crates set out in the shape of a triangle (see below). All the crates were numbered. Can you deduce the number of the crate at the head of the triangle?

```
        ?
     22  16
   13   9   7
  8   5   4   3
```

Sherlock Holmes observed five petty criminals as they cheated at poker in a small tavern one evening. He waited until they had finished playing and were in the process of counting up their winnings before moving in to arrest them. Between them, they had a total of £70. From the following information, can you determine exactly how much each one of them had?

1. Black had £3 more than Andrews.
2. Conn had £3 more than Black.
3. Denny had £6 more than Black.
4. Forbes had £12 more than Andrews.

Following Lord Smedhurst's untimely death, Sherlock Holmes was given the task of tracking down his three long lost sons. His Lordship had left a total of £2,750,000, to be divided between the three of them. His will stated that James, the oldest was to receive three times as much as John, the youngest, while Clive was to receive half the sum allocated to James.

How much would the three sons each receive?

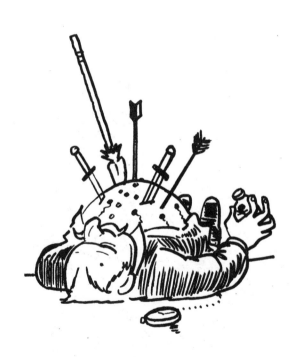

Sherlock Holmes handed Doctor Watson a list of fourteen words. The words were:

TROT	PAGE	RARE
OAT	FOX	RAM
SPAR	ION	TENS
BIT	TILE	REP
MEAL	ROW	

"What am I to do with these?" asked Watson, glancing up at his colleague.

"I want you to make seven seven-letter words from the fourteen by combining two of the words together in each case," replied Holmes.

Can you do it?

Sherlock Holmes was given the special task of protecting a jeweler as he prepared a load of diamonds, pearls, and emeralds for shipment abroad. Holmes stood in the back room of the store as the jeweler weighed the goods on a set of balance scales. Holmes noted that when four emeralds and four pearls were placed on one side of the scales, and three diamonds placed on the other, the scales were perfectly balanced. He also noticed that when three emeralds and two pearls were placed on one side and two diamonds on the other, the scales were equally balanced. This being the case, how many pearls would need to be added to one emerald to balance the scales against two diamonds?

Three men were being held in custody following a post office robbery in which cash, postal orders and stamps were stolen, and a teller was shot and killed. Before being interviewed, the three men agreed to mix up their statements—lies and truth together—to avoid revealing which of them had actually fired the shot that killed the teller. One of the three was a bad liar so it was agreed that he should tell the truth at all times, another would tell one true fact and one lie, while the third would tell lies on all occasions.

Unknown to the three criminals, Sherlock Holmes had overheard this part of their conversation. So when he joined Inspector Lestrade for the interviews, he was able to announce just who the killer was.

Can you?

The three conflicting statements made by the robbers were:

Drummond: I collected the cash. Smith shot the teller.
Smith: Clark collected the stamps and postal orders.
    Drummond shot the teller.
Clark: Smith shot the teller. I collected the cash.

Sherlock Holmes and Doctor Watson raided the small apartment of a petty crook, acting on information that stolen weapons could be found on the premises. In all, four weapons were found. From the following details, can you work out where each was found?

1. The rifle wasn't found in the oven or the kitchen drawer.
2. The shotgun was found after the rifle.
3. The last weapon to be found was discovered in a cupboard.
4. The pistol was found first, but not behind the bookcase.
5. The bayonet was found before the shotgun, but not in the oven.

As they traveled by hansom cab to Scotland Yard, Sherlock Holmes set Doctor Watson the following problem to solve:

Can you identify the missing letter in this sequence of letters: D G C F B ?

Sherlock Holmes and Doctor Watson were traveling to Edinburgh by train from Kings Cross station.

"This is going to be a long, boring journey, Holmes," remarked Watson as they settled into their carriage.

"Then I'll give you something to do to keep yourself occupied," replied Holmes with a smile. "Imagine that you have in front of you a 14 x 14 square grid. Now I want you to tell me how many rectangles, of any size, you can find in the grid."

"Piece of cake," replied Watson. But it was much more difficult than he imagined.

Can you deduce the answer?

Following a robbery, Sherlock Holmes tracked down four criminals, each of whom was carrying something from the robbery when he was caught. From the following information, can you deduce what each of them carried?

1. Neither Mead nor Little had the precious stones.
2. Neither Ford nor Little had the rare stamps.
3. Porter, who didn't have the money, thought that Mead had the oil painting, but he was wrong.
4. Holmes caught the criminals sitting in a cafe where the person with the stamps was sitting to the right of Porter.
5. Ford didn't have the money.

Lord Hemsley looked quite distraught when he called on Sherlock Holmes at his residence, 221b Baker Street. His Lordship had been mugged and lost his cigar case, tie pin, and gold ring, only some 20 minutes before his arrival. He estimated the value of all three items at a combined price of £27,000. If the cigar case was worth ¾ the value of the gold ring, and the tie pin ⅔ the value of the cigar case, what was the value of each item?

After excellent work by Sherlock Holmes, the £122,500 proceeds from a bank robbery were finally traced and recovered. The money had been hidden in three different locations. The unused barn held half the amount of money that was recovered from the warehouse, while the money recovered from the empty apartment was twice as much as that recovered from the warehouse.

Can you work out exactly how much money was recovered from each location?

While visiting Lord Ashworth, Sherlock Holmes inquired about the three wall safes, one on top of the other, on the east wall of the library. Lord Ashworth explained that one held documents, another money, and the third jewelry. He then proceeded to tell Holmes, "The combination of the top safe is 45326, the middle safe is 74017, while the bottom safe is 28?91."

Can you identify the missing number from the combination of the bottom safe?

While working on a case, Sherlock Holmes, Doctor Watson, and Inspector Lestrade all stayed overnight in a Brighton hotel. They had separate rooms on the second floor. Altogether—including Holmes, Watson, and Lestrade—there were four people staying on the second floor, occupying room numbers (reading from left to right at the top of the stairway) 21, 22, 23, and 24. In the morning Holmes was informed by the hotel manager that the other gentleman staying on the second floor had been brutally murdered during the night. From the following information, can you identify the room number of the victim?

1. Watson was to the left of the victim, while Homes was to the right.
2. Lestrade was directly to the right of Watson, but to the left of Holmes.

"How about this for a bargain, Holmes?" said Doctor Watson, as he dropped a large tattered leather case on the desk in front of Holmes. "£120 the lot!"

"Looks a little past it," replied Holmes.

"You're referring to the case, Holmes, but it's the surgeon's instruments contained inside which are the bargain! They cost £118 more than the case, and would cost three times as much if I were to purchase them new."

Can you deduce exactly what Watson would have to pay if he had in fact purchased the instruments new?

Doctor Watson met with four other doctors, each from different cities. From the following information, can you work out which doctor came from which city and how many years he had been practicing medicine?

1. Doctor Brown didn't come from Liverpool or Coventry, nor had he been a doctor for seven years.
2. Doctor Baker had been a doctor for half the amount of time as the doctor from Coventry.
3. The doctor from Edinburgh had been practicing medicine for six years.
4. The doctor from Bristol had been a doctor for 15 years.
5. It was either Doctor Burns or Doctor Wood who had been a doctor for 14 years.
6. Wood had been a doctor for more years than Brown and Burns.

While Sherlock Holmes and Doctor Watson were traveling in a hansom cab toward Scotland Yard, Holmes gave Watson a piece of notepaper. On it was written the following sequence of letters and a clue:

E O E R E ? ?   (NUMBERS)

Can you identify the missing two letters?

In the last month Sherlock Holmes was responsible for sending five men to prison for various offenses. From the clues given below can you deduce the full identity of the five men, give the crime each of them committed and the prison they were sent to after conviction?

1. Andrews committed burglary but was not sent to Brixton or Durham prison.
2. Tom was sent to Dartmoor prison but not for assault.
3. John's was the worst offense—that of murder—but he was not sent to Wandsworth.
4. Neither Stone nor Watson was convicted of assault.
5. James was the horse thief and was not sent to Wandsworth or Brixton prison.
6. David was sent to Wandsworth prison.
7. It was either Jones or Hare who had the first name Robert and neither was the pickpocket.
8. John's surname had only four letters.
9. Hare was sent to Wormwood Scrubs but not for horse theft or assault.

91

ANSWERS

Page	Puzzle	
5	**1**	They were husband and wife.
6	**2**	Moriarty will rob No. 27.
7	**3**	The man informed the robber that the ferry was on its way in—not out.
8	**4**	"I'm going to be shot by a firing squad."
9	**5**	20 minutes past 2
10	**6**	The three men were Fred Bloggs, Archie Doe, and Norman Fiddle.
11	**7**	Box A, 49 matches; box B, 48 matches; box C, 56 matches; box D, 47 matches.
12	8	Holmes's thinking must have been along these lines: If I have a red cap, then Lestrade must have a white, because if both Lestrade and I had red caps—and there are only two red caps—then Watson would know that the cap on his head is a white one. Likewise, Watson would have to have a white cap, or Lestrade would know that the cap on his own head was white. Therefore, I must have a white cap.
13	**9**	"I will steal coins from the postmaster on Monday."
14	**10**	He was her twin brother.
15	**11**	

Name	Nickname	Weapon
O'Shea	Basher	knife
Grant	Knuckles	club
Parker	Buster	crowbar

Page	Puzzle	
16	**12**	Place nine coins in a square to form three rows of three. Then place another coin on top of the first coin in row one, then another coin on top of the second coin in the second row, and finally another coin on top of the third coin in row three. You now have three vertical rows and three horizontal rows of four coins.
17	**13**	6 foot, 6 inches (1.95m)
18	**14**	First, doctor. Second, Holmes. Third, Lestrade. Fourth, accountant.
19	**15**	Hiking boots, £20.50; compass, £2.
20	**16**	Moscow. Istanbul. Copenhagen. Glasgow. Helsinki. Athens. Edinburgh. London. (Disregard Glasgow, which is the only city that has not been a capital, and use the first letter from the others to spell out the name, Michael.)

Page	Puzzle			
21	**17**	Full name	Ward	Husband's Occupation
		Nancy Smithson	2	cab driver
		Audrey Jones	4	undertaker
		Barbara Green	6	doctor
22	**18**	36 minutes.		

21 **17**

Full name	Ward	Husband's Occupation
Nancy Smithson	2	cab driver
Audrey Jones	4	undertaker
Barbara Green	6	doctor

22 **18** 36 minutes.

23 **19** Lady Agatha had gray hair; Lady Jane was the blonde; Lady Davina was the redhead.

24 **20** Holmes was walking north through a train while it was traveling south.

25 **21** Burglar.

26 **22** Five gloves.

27 **23** Holmes juggled the balls as he went across.

28 **24** 68 years old.

29 **25** Prague. Zagreb. Chester. Madrid.

30 **26** Golfing. (Amelia's preferences always began and ended with the same letter.)

31 **27** Lestrade found the crowbar. Watson found the fingerprints. Holmes found the banknotes.

32 **28** Moriarty, 28; Malloy, 14; White, 7.

33 **29** First, criminologists. Second, Scotland Yard. Third, lawyers. Fourth, journalists. Fifth, doctors.

34 **30** 10. 2. 2. 4. 10. (Each of the numbers is worth only half its value.)

35 **31** A fool and his money are soon parted.

36 **32** 1. Gold coin 2. Matches 3. Pen knife 4. Key 5. Pencil 6. Comb

37 **33** Necklace, £140; watch, £80; ring, £120; bracelet, £160.

38 **34** From left to right, Hatchet Jack, Fingers, Greasy Harry, Big Al.

39 **35** 1. Storekeeper 2. Policeman 3. Hairdresser 4. Politician

40 **36** Holmes, 135; Black, 110; Watson, 95; Lestrade, 85.

41 **37** The man was 66 years of age.

42 **38** Both are worth 2. (Value the vowels of each word as follows: A = 0, E = 1, I = 2, O = 3, and U = 4.)

43 **39** Six days.

44 **40**

Mr. Black	Grocer	Able Street
Mrs. Carr	Baker	Bright Street
Mr. Shell	Engineer	Law Street
Mr. Cook	Banker	Hay Street

45 **41**

BENDABLE	HOTSHOT	ROADWORK
SHOPLIFT	BANKNOTE	BREAKFAST
CASTAWAY	OUTLAW	SETBACK
CHARTING		

46 **42** Holmes, 20 minutes; Lestrade, 24 minutes; Watson, 27 minutes.

Page	Puzzle	
47	**43**	Crackpot, yachting, waistcoat, jackknife.
48	**44**	A and B. (The whole sequence spells out Baker Street backwards.)
49	**45**	1. Hermitage, Leningrad. 2. Prado, Madrid. 3. Rijksmuseum, Amsterdam. 4. The National Gallery, Dublin. 5. The Louvre, Paris.
50	**46**	Lance Hart—money Tom Higgins—silver Bob Brown—diamonds Simon Fish—gold
51	**47**	Holmes had His Lordship's staff place two large blocks of ice on the pedestal. The statue was then set down on the blocks and the slings were removed. When the ice melted, the statue sat squarely on the pedestal.
52	**48**	BOOK BOOT COOT COST CAST CASE
53	**49**	Mr. Banks is the butcher, Mr. Baker is the banker, and Mr. Butcher is the baker.
54	**50**	Only one. (From the box labeled DE, remove one stone. If the stone is a diamond, then the other stone has to be a diamond also. Therefore, the box marked EE must be a diamond and an emerald, while the box marked DD must be two emeralds.)
55	**51**	£21.
56	**52**	Tom Smith—butler John Brown—stable boy Jack Jones—chef Tim Small—gardener
57	**53**	21 hours.
58	**54**	95 people each lost £41.
59	**55**	6 rings, 5 rings, and 3 rings.
60	**56**	Probation, abandon, ransacking.
61	**57**	(Reading from left to right) 7 of diamonds, 9 of clubs, Queen of diamonds, 10 of spades, 9 of hearts, 10 of clubs.
62	**58**	John Fern was the murderer.
63	**59**	First, gold lighter. Second, watch chain. Third, cuff links. Fourth, cigar box. Fifth, diamond tie pin.
64	**60**	Recant, nectar, canter, trance.
65	**61**	Portrays Portends Porthole Portable
66	**62**	House numbers 25, 6, and 19.
67	**63**	Ted, 18 years; Martin, 9 years; Henry, 6 years.

Page	Puzzle	

Index